DIVORCE

© Aladdin Books Ltd 1989

Published in the United States in 1990 by
Gloucester Press, 387 Park Avenue South, New York, NY 10016

Printed in Belgium

Editor: Catherine Bradley
Design: Andy Wilkinson, Rob Hillier
Picture research: Cecilia Weston-Baker
Consultant: Pete Sanders

Pete Sanders is the head teacher of an elementary
school. He is working with teachers on personal, social and
health education. Angela Grunsell is an advisory teacher
specializing in development education and resources for the
primary school age range.

The photographs reproduced within this book have been posed
by models or have been obtained from photographic agencies.

ISBN 0-531-17214-7

Library of Congress Catalog
Card Number 89-81604

"LET'S TALK ABOUT"

DIVORCE

ANGELA GRUNSELL

Gloucester Press
London · New York · Toronto · Sydney

"Why talk about divorce?"

Most of us know couples who have decided not to live together any more. You or your friends may have parents who live apart. People often marry for love, but living with someone else can be very difficult. Many couples don't live "happily ever after."

Going through a divorce is hard for everyone involved. Peter had never been so miserable as when his father and mother divorced. He found it hard to talk to anyone about it. But it can help if you talk about what is happening to you during a divorce. Talking can make sense out of confusion. This book aims to help you understand more about divorce.

> Happiness and sadness occur in every family at some time. Good things and new friendships often come out of hard times.

"What is divorce?"

Divorce is the legal end of a marriage. It gives each partner the right and freedom to lead a separate life. Conditions or rules are agreed about how property and money will be shared out and who the children will live with. A divorce settlement divides all the things a couple own jointly. If people cannot agree on fair shares, they have to ask their lawyers to sort it out. If the couple still cannot agree, the case is brought to court where a judge makes the final decision. It is very difficult to work out an agreement that seems fair to both partners, especially when both are bound to have strong feelings. A husband or wife may have to face losing their home and their way of life, as well as losing the person they have cared for or depended on.

Marriages often start out with high hopes, but life together may not match a couple's expectations.

"What happens to the children in a divorce?"

Parents have to agree on who will have custody of each child. Custody means who will take legal responsibility for seeing that the child is fed, clothed, housed and taken care of every day. Visiting arrangements, or access, to the children by the other parent is agreed upon and made to happen by a court.

Sometimes it is clear which of the parents will have the child living with them. But sometimes parents cannot agree what is best – maybe both the mother and father want the child to live with them. Then a social worker or a counselor may try to help the parents to "conciliation," or agreement. He or she will talk with them about what might be the best solution from the child's point of view. If they still cannot agree, a court welfare officer makes a report. Sometimes the children's views are included in this report, along with those of teachers and others who know the child. But this does not always happen.

Partners may decide to separate and get help before they decide on a divorce. They may think their children know what is happening, but they may not have been able to talk to them about it.

9

In many divorces children end up living with their mother. Often mothers have spent more time looking after the children. Most parents will realize divorce is difficult for children.

"Is it my fault?"

"My Dad left home on Friday night, just before the weekend. I couldn't believe it. I thought, if I'd been nicer to him maybe he wouldn't have gone."

You can stop being a husband or wife but you don't stop being a parent. Divorce is about two adults making a change in relationship because things have gone wrong between them. Usually, there is nothing anyone can do to bring parents together if they want to be apart. Sometimes if the parents argue about children and how to treat them, it can be because they both love them very much but cannot agree with each other.

Law courts tend to see the mother as the best person to take care of young children. But that's not always the case. Fathers who live apart may worry that they will lose touch with their children as a result of divorce.

Have you ever come to the end of a close friendship? Once you shared all your secrets but now your friend only annoys you.

"Why do so many people get divorced?"

When two people marry, they hope their love and respect for each other will carry them through difficult times. But this is not always the case. Being with the same partner for life may mean staying together for more than 50 years. Couples separate because they want different things in life. Or they may stop finding each other attractive. Sometimes they argue too much. Difficulties in a marriage can be made worse by lack of money, unemployment, bad housing. Having elderly relatives living with a couple can be hard. Sometimes a couple split up because one of them is in love with someone else.

More people are getting divorced now than in the past. Women can go out to work and no longer have to stay in marriages in which they are unhappy. They can choose to live independently. Every year 300,000 people get married. Every year about 100,000 people get divorced.

13

"They often had fights. But I didn't think it was serious. Why did they get divorced?"

You can't always tell from the outside how happy married people are. Lots of arguments don't necessarily mean an unhappy partnership. Some couples express anger with each other by shouting, breaking things or even hitting each other and then kiss and make up afterwards. Some partners never appear to argue at all; others are cuddling one minute and calling each other names the next. But in a marriage that is ending, while people may fight about small things, the differences between them are at a deeper level. This is what one person said: "We couldn't agree on anything. It got me down and in the end I felt I had to leave."

A divorced parent may need a lot of support from friends and spend a lot of time on the phone.

"Don't my parents care how I feel?"

"Maybe Mom and Dad want to start new lives, but I don't have any choice and no one asked me. It's my life too."

When a marriage breaks up, those involved have to make lots of decisions about how they want to live. There may be lots of anger on both sides and disagreements about money. Just as each spouse is having to get used to living apart, children also have to cope with changes.

Many decisions are outside your control. Other people arrange who you spend time with and when and where you meet. Arrangements for visiting a parent may clash with activities or friendships which mean a great deal to you.

Sometimes a parent may be so caught up in their own concerns that they cannot see their children are upset. They may not be calm enough to listen to you and find out how you are feeling. The parent you live with may complain about the other one and say things which you feel are unfair.

16

Maybe you could talk to a teacher, or a grandparent or a family friend — someone with time to listen to you and help you sort out your feelings.

17

"I don't want anyone to know about the divorce. I sort of feel ashamed."

When your parents are going through a divorce, you may lose your temper with others and worry that your friends might leave you. You may want to spend time alone to come to terms with what has happened. You may not want other people to know about what is going on at home. You may even think that as long as you keep it a secret from everyone, it is not really happening to you.

Your friends may be able to help. Some of them may have been through the experience of having their parents split up. If your friends know, it can help to explain why you might not want to invite them around to your house for a while, but would welcome going to theirs.

> If your parents are divorced, this is an experience you share with lots of other children.

19

"What about the rest of the family?"

"When my daughter-in-law Ruth parted from my son, I didn't see much of my grandchild any more. I missed the fun we used to have doing things together." It can be hard for all family members when a couple divorces – especially grandparents. They don't want to lose that special relationship because their son's or daughter's marriage is over.

Some children find it useful to talk things over with another older member of the family. Their house may be a place where things haven't changed and they have plenty of time to do things with you and listen to you.

"I love visiting grandma's. Everything is just as it has always been. If I stay over she reads to me at bedtime. Mom doesn't often have the time to do that now."

"Why are they still unhappy?"

People don't get over divorce quickly. When parents break up, each may find life very difficult. The parent you are living with may depend on you a great deal, now that she or he is responsible for everything. There is probably less money for all of you because it has to support two households. This may mean less clothes, trips out and treats for you and a lot of worry for your Mom and Dad.

The parent you live with may complain about your other parent's behavior. You don't have to take sides. Divorce is never one partner's fault. But such talk can be very upsetting when you have to see both parents, or you are having to come to terms with the loss of one parent.

> Having one parent looking after you can work out better then having two parents who fight.

"What about visiting my Dad or Mom? When will I do that?"

Winston sees his Dad every Sunday. Jean sees her Mom for a weekend once a month. Assaf sees his Dad on Tuesday, Friday and Saturday evenings.

Moving between two homes can be like living in two different worlds. Each parent has different rules about meals and bedtime. They may have different ideas about what's important. Sometimes parents may try to make up for lost hours with lots of talks or outings when you would rather do something else. It helps to let your parents know how you feel or what you would like to do.

> Ex-partners can become good friends after time apart. This makes going for visits easier. You can begin to enjoy the advantages of two homes and two families.

"Why doesn't Dad come to visit me any more?"

Almost half the children who have divorced parents see the parent they don't live with rarely or not at all. A parent may be so angry with their ex-spouse that she or he doesn't want to allow the children to see him or her. If parents have argued over custody then one parent may feel their ex-spouse may try to keep the child. In some situations a parent may have good reason to mistrust the other.

All this can leave you with many confused feelings and questions about yourself and your parents. There are counseling services that give children or adults the chance to talk to people who have been trained to listen. Losing touch with a parent is a common experience and a very painful one.

> Some people think living apart is better than being unhappy staying together. Others don't.

"Why do parents start new relationships?"

"When Shona moved in with my Dad, I hated her at first. I felt like saying 'You're not my Mom.'" Most adults need lovers and partners. A divorced man or woman usually finds a girlfriend or boyfriend after a while. A divorced parent may decide to live with a new person or get married again.

A thoughtful boyfriend or girlfriend, stepmother or stepfather will realize you need space with your own parent. He or she can also make time to get to know you and show interest in your life. A stepfather or mother can become a close friend and support to you. Through being part of two families you can begin to see you have lots of choices about what is important to you.

> After endings and partings there are also new beginnings which you can be part of.

"What can I do?"

When two people get divorced it causes a lot of upset and distress for their children. Some parents can't talk about what they are going through. Other parents use their children to get at each other. Some parents ask their children to help them. Other parents ask their children for information about their ex-partner. Reading this book may have helped you to understand more about divorce and how some adults and some children feel and behave.

If you are the child of separated parents and need some help or support there are some organizations which can help you. Also, please do not hesitate to speak with your local clergy, a favorite teacher or school counselor, a family friend or any other grown-up that you can trust. If you are upset or find yourself in a situation that is getting out of hand, you can call: National Youth Crisis Hotline 1 - (800) 448-4663.

Addresses for further information

Help, Inc.
638 South Street
Philadelphia, Pennsylvania 19147
(215) 546-7766

Organized "by youth to help youth;" this group maintains a telephone counseling service.

What the words mean?

access means the visiting arrangements made for the parent who does not live with the children.

conciliation is helping a separating couple to agree about how they will share the children in the future.

custody is when one or both parents are given the right to make important decisions about the children's life.

divorce is the legal end of a marriage.

legal means something that is arranged according to a law.

marriage is a legal contract between two people to share their lives and possessions.

separation means a couple decide to live apart.

spouse means a marriage partner.

Index

Photographic Credits:
Cover and pages 8, 12, 14, 17, 24 and 27: Marie-Helene
Bradley; page 4: Anthea Sieveking / Network; pages 6
and 10: Topham Picture Library; pages 18, 21, 22 and
28: Timothy Woodcock.